PIANO | VOCAL | GUITAR • CD   **VOLUME 56**

HAL•LEONARD

Piano PLAY-ALONG

THE 1950s

ISBN-13: 978-1-4234-4955-3
ISBN-10: 1-4234-4955-X

HAL•LEONARD®
CORPORATION
7777 W. BLUEMOUND RD. P.O. BOX 13819 MILWAUKEE, WI 53213

Visit Hal Leonard Online at
www.halleonard.com

BLUEBERRY HILL

Words and Music by AL LEWIS,
LARRY STOCK and VINCENT ROSE

FEVER

Words and Music by JOHN DAVENPORT
and EDDIE COOLEY

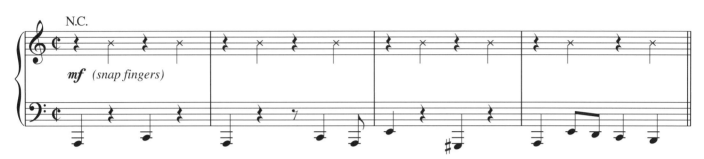

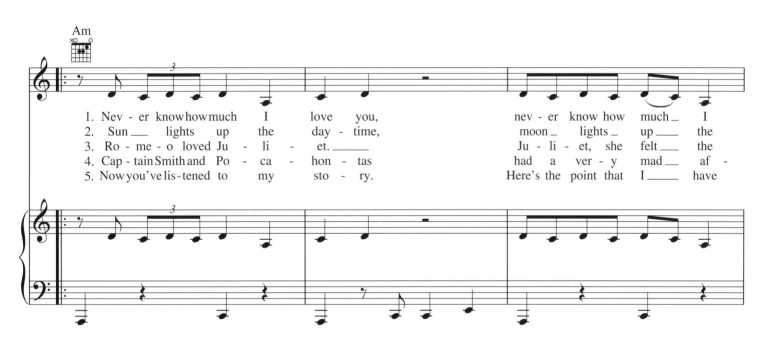

1. Nev - er know how much I love you, nev - er know how much __ I
2. Sun __ lights up the day - time, moon __ lights __ up __ the
3. Ro - me - o loved Ju - li - et. __ Ju - li - et, she felt __ the
4. Cap - tain Smith and Po - ca - hon - tas had a ver - y mad __ af -
5. Now you've lis - tened to my sto - ry. Here's the point that I __ have

care. When you put your arms a - round me, I get a
night. I __ light __ up when you call my name, and you
same. When he put his arms a - round her, he said,
fair. When her dad - dy tried to kill him, she said,
made. Chicks were born to give you fe - ver, be it

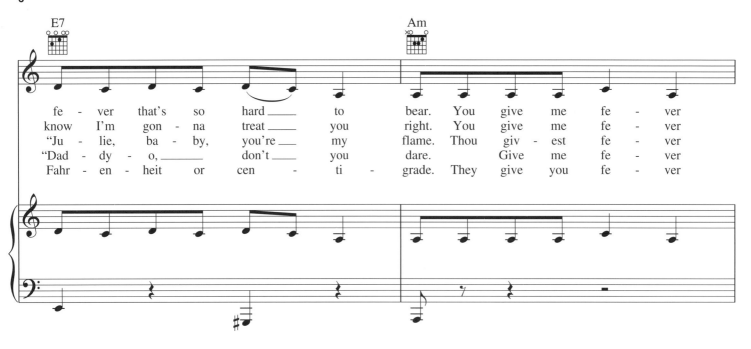

fe - ver that's so hard ____ to bear. You give me fe - ver
know I'm gon - na treat ____ you right. You give me fe - ver
"Ju - lie, ba - by, you're ____ my flame. Thou giv - est fe - ver
"Dad - dy - o, ____ don't ____ you dare. Give me fe - ver
Fahr - en - heit or cen - ti - grade. They give you fe - ver

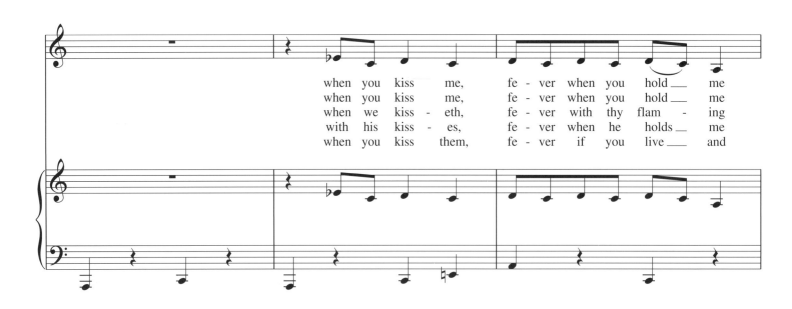

when you kiss me, fe - ver when you hold ____ me
when you kiss me, fe - ver when you hold ____ me
when we kiss - eth, fe - ver with thy flam - ing
with his kiss - es, fe - ver when he holds ____ me
when you kiss them, fe - ver if you live ____ and

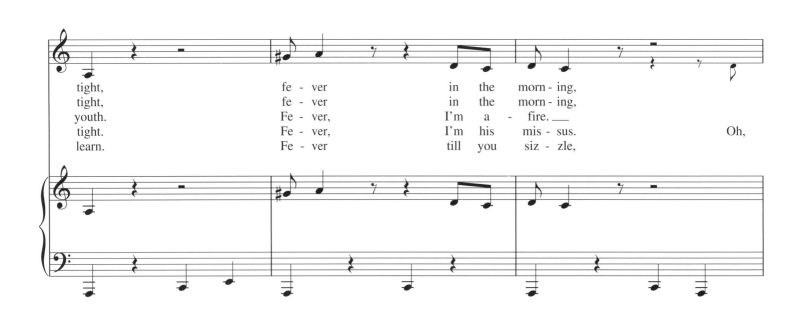

tight, fe - ver in the morn - ing,
tight, fe - ver in the morn - ing,
youth. Fe - ver, I'm a - fire. ____
tight. Fe - ver, I'm his mis - sus.
learn. Fe - ver till you siz - zle, Oh,

DREAM LOVER

Words and Music by
BOBBY DARIN

THE GREAT PRETENDER

Words and Music by
BUCK RAM

Oh, yes, ___ I'm the great pre-tend-er, ___ pre-

tend-in' I'm ___ do-in' well. My need is such, ___ I pre-

tend too much; I'm lone-ly, but no ___ one can tell. Oh,

KANSAS CITY

Words and Music by JERRY LEIBER
and MIKE STOLLER

might take a train, _____ I might take a plane, _____ but
stay with that wom - an I know I'm gon - na die, _____ got - ta

if I have to walk _____ I'm goin' just the same. __ I'm go - in' to
find a brand - new ba - by and that's the rea - son why I'm go - in' to

Kan - sas Cit - y, _____ Kan - sas Cit - y here I

come. _____ They got a

MY PRAYER

Music by GEORGES BOULANGER
Lyric and Musical Adaptation by JIMMY KENNEDY

Moderately slow

When the twi-light is gone _____ and no song-bird is sing - ing, _____

____ when the twi-light is gone _____ you come in-to my

PUT YOUR HEAD ON MY SHOULDER

Words and Music by
PAUL ANKA

MEMORIES ARE MADE OF THIS

Words and Music by RICHARD DEHR,
FRANK MILLER and TERRY GILKYSON